AFTER HOURS
ON MY TRAVELS

FOR PIANO SOLO

PAM WEDGWOOD

FABER *ff* MUSIC

© 2015 by Faber Music Ltd
This edition first published in 2015
Bloomsbury House 74–77 Great Russell Street London WC1B 3DA
Music processed by Jackie Leigh
Cover by Velladesign
Printed in England by Caligraving Ltd
All rights reserved

ISBN10: 0-571-53904-1
EAN13: 978-0-571-53904-8

To buy Faber Music publications or to find out about the full range of titles available
please contact your local retailer or Faber Music sales enquiries:

Faber Music Limited, Burnt Mill, Elizabeth Way, Harlow, CM20 2HX England
Tel: +44 (0)1279 82 89 82   Fax: +44 (0)1279 82 89 83
sales@fabermusic.com   fabermusicstore.com

CONTENTS

LE CAFÉ À CHAMONIX

It was a freezing morning in the Alps and I'd just had my first try at
cross-country skiing (not brilliant). This café served the most welcome coffee ever.

Pam Wedgwood

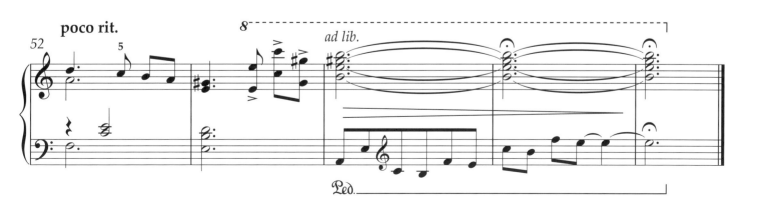

O'BRANIGAN'S BAR

I once cycled from the top to the bottom of Ireland, coming
across a wealth of traditional Irish music in almost every pub!

Pam Wedgwood

DELORES

When my boys were young we spent many summer holidays in a little
white town in southern Spain called Gualchos; Delores was our neighbour there.

Pam Wedgwood

With a lively Latin feel ♩ = 138

CHEZ KATE

I had the most amazing few days staying with my friends in the French Alps.
I wrote this piece for Kate, who is a brilliant cook.

Pam Wedgwood

D.C. al 𝄌
then to Coda   𝄌 CODA

JOHN O'GROATS

Jan de Groote ran the ferry from the Scottish mainland to Orkney and charged one groat.
This piece represents my joy and relief at reaching John O'Groats after two weeks on a bike!

Pam Wedgwood

GERVAISE

This piece is written in memory of Gervaise, an amazing lady who
taught and inspired many musicians throughout her long and interesting life.

Pam Wedgwood

15

THETIS ISLAND

Thetis Island lies off the coast of British Columbia, Canada; I visited great friends on the island many times.
Unfortunately one of my greatest friends died there after a fight with cancer; this is written in his memory.

Pam Wedgwood

FREEDOM BLUES

I wrote this piece following a visit to Robin Island, where Nelson Mandela was captive for many years.
I have huge respect for his years of suffering and the eventual joy and freedom he achieved.

Pam Wedgwood

Slow blues ♩ = 72

THE SPIRIT OF POHUTUKAWA

The pohutukawa tree is New Zealand's version of a Christmas tree. It produces huge blooms of crimson flowers and is found clinging to steep hillsides. The best-known pohutukawa tree can be found in Cape Reinga, a place of great spiritual significance to the Maori people.

Pam Wedgwood

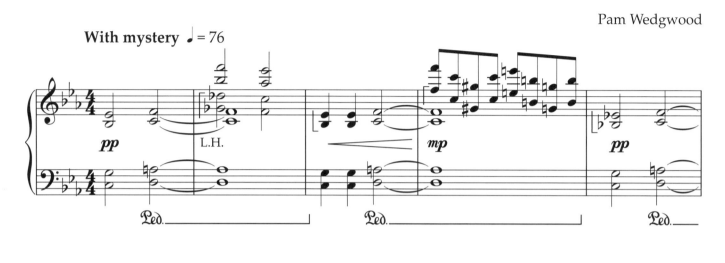

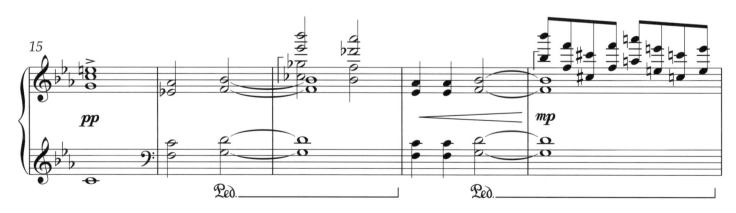

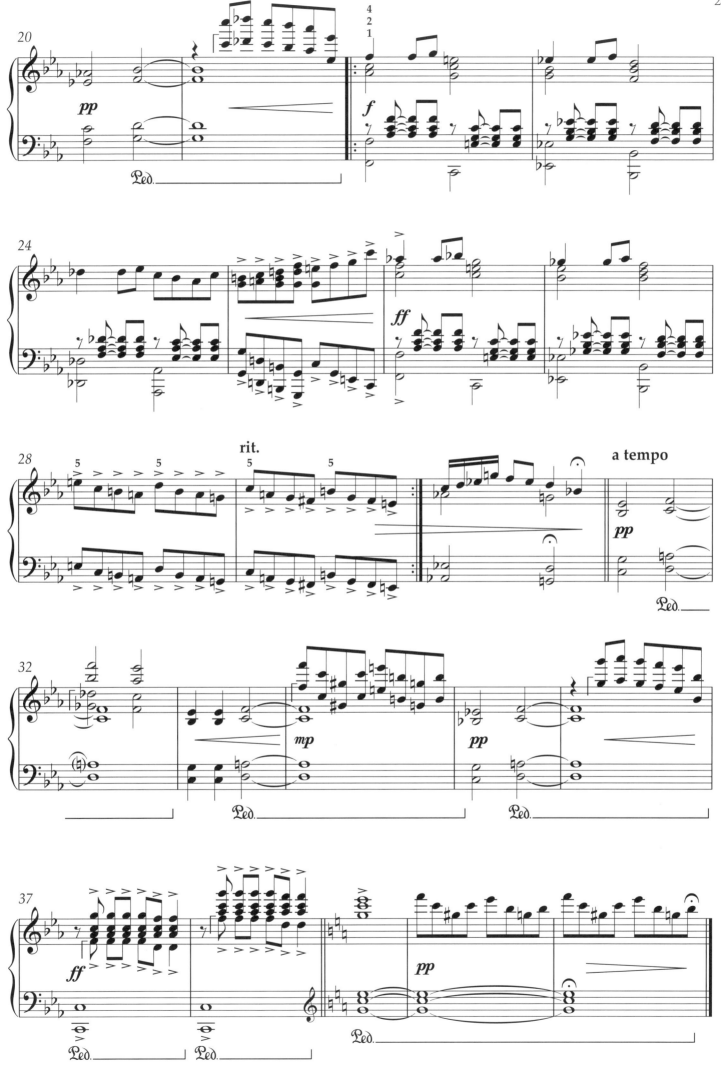

CITY LIGHTS

The changing faces of a vibrant city

Sydney is my favourite city in Australia. To me it represents beach heaven,
food heaven, coffee heaven, recreation heaven and cultural heaven!

Day-break *(first time)*

Twilight *(second time)*

Pam Wedgwood

Slow and dreamy ♩ = 86

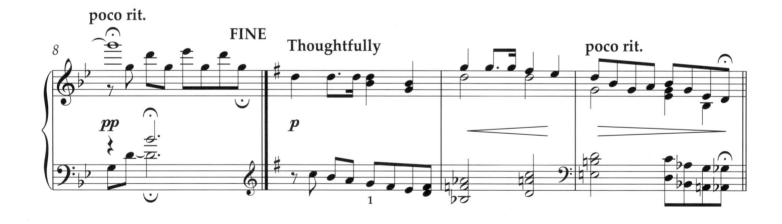

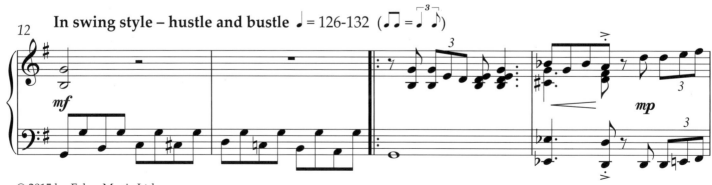

ABEL TASMAN

Crystal Waters

Abel Tasman is a national park located at the north end of New Zealand's South Island.
I was lucky enough to spend six glorious weeks in this beautiful place.

Pam Wedgwood

LE POULET

Le poulet is a beautiful chalet in Les Houches in France. This is about the chalet dog, Rosie!

Pam Wedgwood

At last, a juicy stick!

slowing down

a tempo (not swung)

FREEDOM WALK

This piece was inspired by a wonderful trip to South Africa
and many years of listening to 'Graceland' (Paul Simon).

Pam Wedgwood